Encore of the Fading Light

Roisin Rzeznik

Contact: Roisin Rzeznik; RoRzeznik Publishing: RoRzeznik@yahoo.com

FOR

YAHWEH
The Love of our life

VAL KILMER

"For you and me, Today is; though as surely as yesterday has passed, we know not what, or if tomorrow shall be; yet our thanks is to God Almighty today has come, for you and me." -Roisin Rzeznik

CONTENTS

ACKNOWLEDGMENTS

You know who you are, Thank You; I Love You!

Apple Tree Boy

He has no one- no one he can trust

He covers his pain with a liquid rush

As he crawls inside himself…

He tries to fool the world-

Denying Love's touch

Doesn't he know; Doesn't he know

Oh don't you know

Your eyes can't lie to Love

Your eyes can't lie to Love

Be brave- Have Courage

No need to hide your scars

I love you for who you are

I love you just the way you are

Your eyes can't lie to Love

Your eyes can't lie to love

There is hope from above

An eternal promise

A Hero is on His way

He hears us when we pray

Love-Love will you save the day

He knocks upon your door

Oh, won't you let him in

Love-Let Him in

Love will win

Your eyes can't lie to Love

Your eyes can't lie to Love

Oh Lord cradle this one in your arms like a child

Oh Lord I love him

The world has left him so defiled

Oh Lord love him like I do

I'm leaving it all up to You

Oh Lord cradle this one in your arms tonight

I remember him undefiled

Don't let him lose this fight

Break him and facet him how you must

Whatever it takes

Lord in you, I put my trust

He's so alone

He's a long long-way from home

From ashes to ashes

Your eyes can't lie to Love

Your eyes can't lie to Love

Scared and cold

His eternal light has begun to dim

He fears his soul is fading

Oh Lord won't you save him

He's knocking-Let Him in

He's so alone

He's a long long-way from home

He longs for home

Dust to dust

Your eyes can't lie to Love

Your eyes just can't lie to Love

Hey

Don't you know

Hey

You know

I Love You

Lonely Prayer

Let me love you

Meet me halfway

Let me love you

Don't do it

Don't let it slip away

Hold me close now

Please don't choose to go

I can't take you leaving

Oh, I love you

I love you, I love…

Don't do it

Don't leave me sighing

Please don't leave me crying

A love, so essential

There's no denying

Last time-I died

Didn't you hear me screaming

As I cried

"No, no, no, please don't let me go!"

Swallowed in time

Devoured by the mind

Complete vertigo

Don't do it

Don't throw it all away

I don't want to be over you

Throw away your pride

Help me come alive

I don't want to live without you

Don't hide your love inside

Hold me close now

Don't let me go!

Love me forever

Oh- you know!

You know!

Follow Me

Though our lives took different roads

We end up on the same path

Me looking out for you

You watching my back

If you get there before I do,

Know I'm not far behind

Keep going- Don't wait

I'll meet you at the end of time

Keep looking up

Know we are headed the right way

Time cannot destroy us

Nor can the games people play

I've loved you always

Know I'm not afraid

Keep your eyes on the Lord

He is the only way

Wisdom

Wisdom in the words

I hear you whisper in the night

Wisdom in your words

Telling me I can

Assuring me everything will be alright

Kind is your voice

You promise no lies

I feel the beauty of your heart

You tell me I have a choice

I realize,

You honor my soul

Dignified grace

Why I call you friend

Dignified Grace

Wisdom Within

Listen-Up Friend

I thought I found a friend

A friend in you

I started to trust

Trust in you

I thought you were real

You didn't know it

You didn't know

I read you from across the room

Last night

Your put-down

I guess it made you feel pretty tight

I read you from across the room

Ok, you're cool now

Taken in by the illusion of the prism pristine

All for a rhinestone queen

I can see now

Can you hear me now

(Listen up)

No longer blind

I can see now

You're so transparent

(Oh so transparent)

I can see you're a, "What's in it for me" now

You're so transparent

I want to tell you to your face

I'm not ashamed-to walk in His grace

You didn't know it

You didn't know

I came a long way to support you

I was there for you

An offer in hand for you

The illusion of the prism got the best

The best of you

No longer peering through

Rose-colored lenses removed

I see the truth now

It's no use

You're an imposter

I can see now

Can you hear me now

(Listen up)

No longer blind

I can see now

You're not real

You're so transparent

(Oh so transparent)

You're a, "What's in it for me" now

You're so transparent

I want to tell you to your face

I'm not ashamed- I walk in His grace

The Dream

The words just won't come today

The tears fall like a cold rain

 Burned by love

By its unforgiving flame

Robbed by desire

Once upon a time

I believed

I believed in Love

Like all little girls

I had a dream

 A dream of love

Choked by magic

Cinderella

I stood before my dream

He let me walk away

Forever

Tears stream

Drowned in hope

Tears don't wash away the pain

Forever unclean

Unworthy of desire

Burned by love

Returned to the mire

Abandoned by faith

A head hung in shame-

Never again

Will my heart play

Burned by love

To him a game

Gored by love

Smothered

by the dream

Abandoned

by the dream

Broken

by the dream

Shattered

by my dream

The dream

Himself

Open Letter to the Past

Open letter to the Past:

Heart of Stone,

I saw a vision of how you'd be-

If it would have played out differently.

You'd be lonesome just like me.

I saw you sitting,

Deep in thought-

Lost and Alone

It left me wondering

Where you'd call home.

I always thought if...

I were in your arms I'd be home

My eyes swell and I'm filled with pride when I see you

All I ever wanted was to feel your hand in mine.

If things were different

If I peeled the layers back,

After all these years,

What would be revealed.

Would you still be the one I call home;

Would you be the man, I thought you'd always be

Have the years; the wealth; and your name

Driven that man from your soul.

Are you still the same.

Through the years, it's caused me so much pain

Destine to be alone.

Your success outweighed it all.

I never wanted to search for something new.

I was content just being proud of you.

I always thought I needed you.

I wanted the Love in your heart,

Ever present on your lips.

I wanted to feel the tenderness of your touch

Forever.

The pain was so unpleasant;

I didn't want to stare into vacant eyes.

I want to see your soul.

Life's "little" shortcut still hasn't brought me home.

What happens to love when every ounce of hope is gone.

I looked into the mirror;

What I had and my future in an instant- was gone.

Who gave anyone the right to take that from me

All for loving you.

What do I have to show for all these years- nothing

Nothing but splinters, slivers, dust, and endless tears.

Does this heart have to remain heavy.

I never wanted anyone but you.

I never wanted more than your heart could give.

How could I feel love;

A love so strong.

How could that love not be real;

How could that love not be true.

I've been injured; I've been wronged

And the criminal...calls himself justified.

Why does my heart have to remain this heavy.

I never wanted more than you.

I've never cared for what comes with money.

How I'd hoped for you

To be set free

What I've held onto all these years.

All that love-all those dreams

Are they nothing.

I couldn't bear the thought.

I would have waited forever

Silent

Are you telling me all these things...

Were never more than

Splinters, slivers, dust, and tears.

How could I ever find someone;

Someone that makes it feel all right,

It was so hard to face the lonely nights...

Then I found myself,

Tear drenched without a prayer,

With only my final breath left to take;

My love for you, I placed on the altar in God's care.

Prone with my face in the dirt

I begged God for His mercy upon you;

I begged Him for your safety and that of your soul's.

I begged Him to pull you through.

Now that I know-

I know,

Myself.

I am angry.

I am angry with myself.

I forgive you; it wasn't your fault.

These choices weren't yours to make.

I loved you freely; it was my choice.

I'd do it again without question;

This was my cross to bear.

I'd rather die than be eternally without you.

This is why, I walked away;

My love for you remains.

If ever your heart changes, you know where to find me,

I'll continue to pray for you far beyond my dying day

I want for you what I've found.

A place where love never fades away.

Now I know my heart won't remain heavy.

But it still hurts without you my friend.

I miss you each and every day.

I guess some things never change.

Though I don't know why; I've been...

Saved by the hand of God.

By the love of Christ, Himself.

Through His mercy and beautiful grace.

I know from this dream I wake,

To a brighter dawn.

-Roisin

Heart and Soul

I'm never alone

I carry you within

In my dreams

You are set free

Heart and soul

In your arms

I know a home

When daylight comes

And you return to flesh

Though I wake without you

Forest and Irish clover linger

I am lost without you

I close my eyes

And trace your face

I remember

Together again

Beyond time

Your hair through my fingers

Your breath, life itself

Your heartbeat like thunder

Your lips upon mine sustain me

You love like no other

I need your love

Lonely without you

For I know sweet surrender

Outside of time

Bravo! Bravo!

Funny how

The bullies

Have to be heard…

How they

Have to

Let you know

You're within

Their grasp

They deliver

Their words

To prove

To you

They can

Move past

Your lines

Your lines

Of

Love

All that they think you've drawn

And

If you don't

Comply

They'll erase what you love

And

Take it all away

And

All that you own

How absurd

You think me a fool

Nestled down

For a long winter's nap

Ready to step aside

For

Love

And

You wake me

For what

To tell me

You're

Afraid

I'll draw first-blood

I don't draw first-blood

I leave that up to you

Whatever happened to…

Good old fashion ground rules

I know

What I love

And

I love

What I do

And

I know

What I've earned

And

I know

What I'd do

For

Love…

My lines clearly defined

Sculpted so you'd know

When you're

Holding the knife to his throat

Another needle to his arm

Crossing my lines of love

Will only bring you down

Exchange of Enlightenment

I know the truth

It'll hurt me

I pretend

I pretend I cannot see

The truth

It already hurt me

God rescued me

I am a shell

Of whom I should have been

Yet I pretend

Because I know

I cannot see

Love has only hurt me

God picked me up

When I couldn't run

Love

A nightmare

Brought to life

I could no longer see

The only One that truly loves me

He calls me by name

I break His heart just the same

If I looked

I could see it in His eyes

Yet He pretends

He lets me believe

I cannot see

Exactly

What it means

This game love played

The damage love has done

I pretend I cannot see

I pretend love remains

I tell myself

I could be Love's queen

Yet I know

God picked me up

When I could not run

I'm just a means

I pretend I can't see

The nightmare

Myself a pawn

Worthless in Love's eyes

Useless

Unless I'm gain

Reach

Reach for me

I've come so far

To hold your hand

All my life

Or so it seems

You've been the only man

I've waited for you

Through good and bad

Waiting for that one moment

For a split second

For it to come around

Again

For my chance

To let you know

Who I am

And here we are

Now we know

It's just a dream

I stand before you

But

The world won't let us be

It'll never be the same

I couldn't go

I couldn't ask you to stay

It was your decision to make

I had waited so long

It was then I saw it

Revealing itself

Some twisted plan

Before I could reach you;

I couldn't reach you

I must have let you down

I wanted you to take my hand

All I could do was turnaround

I couldn't let you know

I couldn't let you go down

For my sake

Since that moment

I haven't had one free of pain

I think you thought

And felt

The same

But yet

You let me walk away

Had I said,

Reach for me

I've come so far

To hold your hand

It will never come around again…

Within You

I saw

You

As a child

Today

Beside yourself

You sat alone

The thick mud

Washed from my eyes

In the white snow

I could see

A reflection

Of me

In your eyes

I could feel your heart

I've seen

Love

In a state of flux

Love

In constant motion

Within you

Now I see

Love in total

You make it easy

To believe

Love is alive

Chosen

I want to hear it

Tell me you've chosen

Closing my eyes

Waves crash against the wall

IF I dream louder

Can I make you appear

Amid the roar

I hear your voice

As I reach out

I stretch my arms wide

Standing here, I am ready to embrace you

I know you've chosen

Now I disappear

The cold spray drenches me

If I wish harder will I feel you

I want to be near you

Rescue Me from living on the edge

Define me beyond the fray

The drum is still beating out of time

Before they extinguish my light

If I pray long enough

Will it make everything all right

Chosen one will you save me

Before the morning light

I know you've chosen

Roisin Rzeznik

Last Night

I feel like I've been waiting

Waiting so long

For you to catch up to me

For you to wake up

For you to finally see

For you to hear my song

When I walked away

I thought you'd follow

When it should be easier now

It has become a deeper misery

It gets harder and harder every day

Loving you

It doesn't get easier

The price only steeper to pay

It's only easier now to paint the target on my own head

Right above my eyes

They'd be doing me a favor then

My pain gone

I know

If I go

They'll never see the light of day

Before my body is cold

They'll be wishing they were dead

And you'll be free to leave the game

I will never leave it without you

I jumped in for you

With no regret, no retreat, and no compromise

I've seen the love you have in your eyes

Was this a love never meant to be

Last night I could feel your pain

My Soul Cried

It cried out in horror screaming your name

In that moment the hardest part is not knowing

Are you dead, alive, or are you laying on the ground

Fighting to survive

Each time it's like dying again

Tell me it's not all in vain

This choice I made

For love to remain

Can't you feel me

Like I feel you

Can't you hear my soul calling out your name

When will you walk down this road

It leads you from destruction

I thought our love was true

I thought you'd come to me

I hate this game

There is no one to comfort me

There is no one to carry my pain

Who is willing to comfort me

To this pain I can see no end

Sitting here sobbing once again

And then

Outside my window I could see him

In the morning light

Bravely he came and sat

With a song in his heart just for me

Ruffled feathers for a hat

A Bold and Beautiful Blue Jay

He was begging me to finally see

He's the one who has come to comfort me

...From A Different Cup

Roisin Rzeznik

In Your Arms

In your arms

Do you think

I can heal you

Do you think

You can

Do the same

I wonder IF you touch me

Will what you feel be the same

Do you think

You can heal me

Do you think

I can

Do the same

Advice for a Friend

(Walk Away)

Walk Away

Walk Away

Is what my conscience says

Walk Away

Before you care

My advice to you

When all I really want is to roll-over

And see you there...

Walk Away

Tonight II

I am Miserable

There is not enough

Irish Whiskey

In the world

to drive the loneliness from my soul

The emptiness of my heart

Drives my life to find true love

the walls are closing in

on the lies of happiness

the walls that haven't already crumbled

tonight it's hard to be a Christian

surrounded by politics

and even more hypocrites

it's hard not to be in control

it's hard to have faith

prayer doesn't always come easy

it doesn't always protect from hate

it's hard to trust

In what I can't see

tonight it's hard to be good

and not just be in it for me

it's hard to see a future

it's hard to see the light

it's hard

so hard to be still and know…

Everything is going to be alright

When I'm choking on regret

That I've stored for years

I'm angry,

there's no one to be angry with

I think I hate him

for watching me walk away

for not saving me…

Time and time again

for letting me throw it all away

Then…

Now…

for not being real

for taking my friend

for leaving me with…

No one else

Alone to carry the pain

and there is no one

no one to wipe the tears

there's no one to blame

for this sea of endless pain

for my wasted years…

there is no way out

without the choices I've made

I scream for fairness

But it's never been

I scream for justice

But it feels at a loss,

My friend

I've been cut off;

It's all been taken away

Again

And again

And again

For needing…

Love and affection

For not wanting to go with the flow

For not being someone I'm not

For not settling

For not being silent

For not letting go

I scream for love

Its eyes are vacant

Its kiss…

Resides with someone else

Its heart and arms are absent

It's blind and deaf

Straight through to the core

~

A soul no more

it sings its own sad song

I know

It's not him

Not anymore

It proclaims it's done nothing wrong

It watches me as I choke some more

Tonight

If I could I'd run from everything

Even though...

It would be better to choke even more

The only place I'll run tonight is

Into the arms of my Savior

As I lay myself down

On the cold floor

And choke some more

I know

The whiskey only adds flavor

To a bitter pill

It's hard to be a Christian

But somehow

the light always

Returns

I know

I won't be alone

As I choke some more

At least

This way

I know

I'm alive

The loneliness Burns

It's worse than before

Inside

You...

I saw you

In the crowd

When he turned around

He had your face

I looked away

I looked around

Then I looked again

To see you

Look away

When he turned toward me

He had his own

Again

The visage had changed

"And the band played on…"

Where were you, when the world stopped?

Reckless Epic

Reckless-Epic

How do you feel

Did you bother to ask for truth

I just bought the lies you sold

How does it feel

To bring down someone's world

Fair is fair

Call it what you like

Can't you see

I want the truth

You sold me

No second thought

You took the money

What's it like selling out

You blinded my way

I trusted your everything

You sold me out

Twice

With a wave

You sent me to my grave

To bring down the house

Spineless snake

You gave me up

Gave me over to the enemy

Trusting you

My mistake

Sold me straight-faced

Wanted me lost

Without a trace…

Did you bother to ask for truth

You just bought their lies

I lived for you-I died for you

There's no beauty in betrayal

Did you bother to ask for truth

I loved you

Literal betrayal

Hurt so much

Keep your fame

I have my faith

I have the Word

I don't need your world of hate

I won't waste my time

Wounds that never heal

Was it worth it

Removing my life's breath

You should have torn my heart

Straight from my chest

Did you enjoy the money

I'm still here with voices in my head,

Now you are the song lyric honey...

You're still selling out

Fair is fair

How do you feel

Was it worth it

Do you enjoy every penny

The Truth

It was real

Love

I'm begging you for truth

That's what I was after

I never thought twice

I wanted you

Just as you were

Happily Ever After

I liked you better as a pauper

I'm begging you for the truth

Fair is fair

Keep your fortune

Keep your world

Mine is among the stars

My love for you has never wavered

Forgiven now

Take a good look at who you are

I pray you find Jesus…

You'll know on site

We have matching scars

Artificial Royalty

You took it all

To appease

Your filthy soul

Effortlessly

Sacred

To me

To you

Penny-candy

Golden-fruit

And

Beauty

Became

Rotting flesh

In your hands

For a price

You traded my soul

Untouchable

I thought I knew you

Speechless

You left me wanting

A new you

I thought there was none

Like you

Now I know

I don't want to be an empty soul

Give me Jesus

Give me Jesus

Dream Catcher

On the mirror

Hands lain

A Cross

Face gently pressing upon it

Against its cold surface

Against all odds

I am here

My breath shows

Quickening now

Skipping a beat

My heart leaps

I breathe deep

I wake

Sweat drenched

Prayer beads

In my clenched fist

Breathe deep

It's not yet won

Check again

First the safeguards

Then the clock

Its hands never seem to move

Pause

Breathe deep

The battle is real

I promise you

Distant wail

Moving closer

Check again

Prayer beads

Daylight hasn't come

Closing my eyes

I pray for you

I pray for daylight

Pause

Breathe deep

The battle is real

We begin again

I promise you

We begin again

Pause

Breathe deep

The battle is real

Poem for David

Human hearts So often Break

Some Love

Like Green Grass

In Winter fades To Brown

Or Burns Quickly

Like Lightning From a Storm

There is No Way to Explain

But Like The Green Grass of Spring

Some Love

Is Made to Rejuvenate

Roisin Rzeznik

When Dreams Collide

The sun's glare

Cuts through

The cool air

It warms as it

Slightly blinds;

The gulls dance

As they soar

Above the highway ribbon;

the rhythm

and

the rhymes

Platform Pleasantry Unaware

Ascending

I feel you first

Then I see you appear

Watching from a distance

I see your form outlined

Against the sky

Distant from everyone near

What is it

That I feel in the air

I'm too far away to scream

I can only raise my hand

With a sign

As I see you standing there

Then you disappear

I come closer

I come to you

You're nowhere to be found

I wait...

But I'm not part of this forest

I'm not a tree

I could never be

I leave

But not without a promise

Between you and me

Something we share

I hope next time

You'll see…Me

Standing there

Writing these lines

To tell you how much

 I care

Back at a distance

You re-emerge

Hiding my tears

I watch you

Ascending the stairs

Wrapped in a cloak

High and serene

Looking out from your watchtower

What a dream…

If you'd be looking for me

I'd run into your arms

You carry yourself

Like royalty

Having just stepped from a dream

Stepping back through

From where you came

I watch you again

As you show the world

Your special flair

That's why I came

To see you

Shine again

I count myself privileged

To be among

The many

Even

The mice and men

Roisin Rzeznik

Nothing But You

I don't believe in wishes

I don't believe in dreams come true

I find myself believing in nothing

Nothing but you

Maybe you were heaven sent

Wrapped in a prayer

Carried by a dream

in an altered state

I know you're there

You make me feel

Even when I wouldn't

I see you

Reflected in my eyes

You cover me

Even when you shouldn't

I feel your light

You make it all look simple

I see now

It's true

Nothing but you

I don't believe in wishes

I don't believe in dreams come true

I find myself believing in nothing

Nothing but you

There is no one

Like you

You're the kind

I've dreamt about

The kind

I know doesn't exist…

I see you now even when I shouldn't

Wherever I go

You make me want to believe

I hear myself saying

It's true

Tell me are you all show

Do you believe

Have you ever let go

Nothing but you

I don't believe in wishes

I don't believe in dreams come true

I find myself believing in nothing

Nothing but you

The Fool

Have you ever played the fool

Believed in someone

So much

I believed

In him

With all my heart

Deep within my soul

Blind to truth

I believed

So sure

I believed

It was love

It was truth

So sure…

I am

Am I the fool

You and Me

He shined so bright for a time

Then he lost

The girl and the rhyme

Rhyme for me

Baby rhyme for me

I'll ask you

Baby rhyme for me

One more time

I'll tell you

He shined

He shined so bright

Then he lost

The girl, the rhythm, and the fight

Once again

Like a child I see

I see you in my mind

We're like children

You and me

"Come play with me!"

Baby will you rhyme with me

Before we run out of time

Let's make the world one big rhyme

You and me

Sir William

Sir William

A gallant man

Slays devil, demon, dark angel

And the like

With bare hand

Brave defender

Always

On alert

To protect

Fellow Knight

And Lady

Alike

Judging not those he saves

From the hands of Beelzebub

and his fatal games

Sir William

An open book

His soul's passion constant

His heart a bold brook

In these days dreams die

Plots unfold

Unmasked by Sir William's hand

Darkness is revealed

His light shines through

To remind me

Christ Prevails

Words

Do you remember

The words

That brought me to you

It's the only way I could reach you

It's the only way I could keep you

I kept it to myself

Between you and me

No One Else

Seems so long ago

You told me

Taste and see

The Lord is good

He's been so good to me

The one way to reach me

The one way to keep me

Constantly changing

From whence the two words came

The original

Name and Place

Always remain

The same

Seek me

Speak to me

At first I saw you

I called

But

Could not speak

For me

There was never anyone else

As time passed

I missed my chance

My heart

I couldn't tell you

How much I needed you

I couldn't speak

 I couldn't seek

Always afraid

Always afraid I couldn't play the part

Peace

I had nothing else

Just a mate

What comes with age?

A message

To which you should relate

The price I paid

I'd pay it again

And again

For you,

My Friend

You didn't know

They took it all away

They took me

Away from you

The fragrance

A memory

Seeing double

Never alone

There was always someone else

X-files

A reflection

A tone

I couldn't have poured it out

"**Is** tú mo ghrá!"

I couldn't reach you

I should have dropped to my knees

"**Is** tú mo ghrá!"

Forever I'll remain

Without you

Incomplete

Out of our hands

Under lock and key

Keep it

Keep it to yourself

Always

Between you and me…

To Be Seen and Not Heard

To be seen and Not Heard

Be as silent as you want to be

I can feel you there

Just like you are laying there

Next to me

But silence for now

Is not for me…

Even if your words are not meant for me

I still want to dream…

I spent too many years in the darkness

A different silence

Too many years

In a lost city

The city of despair

I want to speak

Until I lose my voice

Or when my heart dies…

I only want to be silent again

When I'm in your arms

The arms of a friend

When I finally know

That you really care

I'll be silent

In your arms

I dream…

You hide me away

From the darkness

From the city of despair

Take me further away

From this lost city

Take me somewhere…

A place for just you with me

Take me there

From the darkness into the light

Away from the nightmare

Away from the settled for

To a place…

The place

Where neither of us need to speak

To be heard and not seen

Roisin Rzeznik

Encore of the Fading Light

As the light fades

The looming storm approaches

Kicking up the wind

Its warm and sultry caress

Eases my pain

The shadows in the sky intensify

The clouds contrast the moon

Autumn colors blend

Into the mist

Alone

I sit

Isolated

But not entombed

Lightning strikes

A moment frozen in time

Reds and purples mix into grey

Electric light crosses the sky

The pain lifts

And travels away

Becoming part of the dimness

My senses stir

Wide awake

I realize I am

Your Princess

Enveloped in the warmth

Of understanding

On the breeze

I feel you

Gently whisper, your name

It's safe now

I hear thunder approaching again

I Am

Undisturbed

By its rumble and clamor

Rolling across the field

Growing louder

It lulls me

The distance closes

Natural light and colors

Return

Under the canopy of midnight grey

Dancing...

ABOUT THE AUTHOR

Roisin Rzeznik

Roisin Rzeznik is best known by her pseudonym Roisin (Van gogh-Rzeznik). She is a Midwest, Milwaukee, Chicago area artist, writer, photographer, pragmatic philosopher, activist, and humanitarian. She has four children whom are now grown and a grandson.

She enjoys creating....

Roisin is a versatile artist working with many mediums and experimental techniques...most prevalent are her paintings and an occasional block print or rare drawing. Her focus is on contemporary art, abstract expressionism, research, visual rhyme, and poetry.

A tremendous lover of the archaic, prose, and art world-wide. The artist was inspired at an early age by her mentors and their willingness to indulge, experiment, and instruct in a broad, diverse, and eclectic range of art, technique, and philosophy.

Over the years Roisin has spent her time highlighting Fair Trade, fighting for human rights, women's rights, children's rights, racial congruity, the abolition of extreme poverty, Aids, Malaria, human trafficking, and Genocide.

Roisin is known for often crediting her greatest loves as influences including God Himself; music as her muse and those whom create it.

Roisin harbors a deep belief that, "Global Peace and Unity are achievable; They are a tangible gift from the Almighty."

* 9 7 8 0 9 8 9 2 1 4 2 0 9 *